Original title:
Through the Living Room Door

Copyright © 2025 Creative Arts Management OÜ
All rights reserved.

Author: Nolan Kingsley
ISBN HARDBACK: 978-1-80587-067-8
ISBN PAPERBACK: 978-1-80587-537-6

Emblem of Connectedness

In the corner a cat surveys,
As the kids form their wild maze.
Mom's knitting with laughter in tow,
While the dog steals socks, oh no!

Emblem of Connectedness

Dad's lost again in the couch,
Remote buried deep, what a grouch.
The popcorn pops, it's a delight,
As the chaos grows, we take flight.

The Depth of Home

Grandpa reminisces with glee,
Of the wild times that used to be.
The family photo fights the dust,
Each snapshot filled with laugh and trust.

The Depth of Home

The air's a blend of joy and snack,
Finding marbles under the rack.
The walls echo with our shared plight,
In this playful chaos, we unite.

Unseen Threads

Strings of laughter pull us tight,
In the glow of the evening light.
Mom's wings flapping with a flair,
As we dance without a care.

Unseen Threads

Cousins laughing, a wild parade,
Hiding away in the home-made shade.
The game of tag erupts once more,
As the sun dips behind our door.

Threshold of Whispers

A cat perched high, surveying the scene,
As guests slip in, a comical routine.
With snacks in hand, they try to be sly,
But a rogue pizza slice makes them all cry.

Laughter erupts like popcorn in air,
As tales are spun with whimsical flair.
The couch is a throne, where stories collide,
While socks on the floor play hide and seek wide.

The Veil of Homecoming

In comes Uncle Bob, hat askew,
He tripped on a rug, such a sight to view.
With a grin, he stands, dusts off his shoe,
And claims it's a dance move, not something he blew.

A dog darts past with a squeaky toy,
While Grandma winks, full of joy.
She's got cookies galore, and they're hot off the tray,
But melted chocolate, oh, it made quite a display!

Shadows on the Welcome Mat

Footprints smudge where the sunbeam hides,
As cousins emerge, laughter their guide.
One's in a cape, flying down the hall,
While others just nibble, playing it small.

The TV's a backdrop for our grand circus,
As we swap silly jokes and dance just for us.
A quick dash for snacks, balancing plates,
Who knew the living room could tempt such fates?

Glances from the Entryway

A sneeze comes forth, as Grandma will shout,
"You need to stop bringing the pollen about!"
Then, with a chuckle, she joins in the fray,
Waving her hands like it's some cabaret.

Dad's telling a story, it's long and bizarre,
With sound effects that could rival a car.
Mom's rolling her eyes, but she can't help but grin,
As we all dive in for the thick of the din.

A Warm Embrace

A cat on the couch, so snug and tight,
It snores like a bear, what a silly sight!
The dog steals the chips, it's quite the affair,
We laugh at the chaos, not a single care.

The grandkids run riot, their giggles ring clear,
As popcorn flies high, drawing laughter near.
A dance with the broom, in bright plaid pajamas,
We shimmy and shake, to old-time anthems.

The Space Between Us

Two chairs sit apart, but we still connect,
His jokes hit the mark, and what did I expect?
With a wink and a grin, he raises a brow,
I snort as he quips, a fine laugh we allow.

The coffee spills over as the tales unfold,
Of trips gone awry, and funny things told.
Between sips and bites, our laughter ignites,
Creating a warmth on the chilly nights.

Moments in the Air

The clock ticks loudly, time hangs on its wall,
Yet laughter tumbles free, like leaves in the fall.
A memory formed, with stories so bright,
It dances like shadows in soft, glowing light.

Moments that shimmer, like stars in the night,
We chase after giggles, with pure delight.
In every quick glance, and every shared laugh,
We weave a bright tapestry, our joyous craft.

Laughter Between Walls

The wallpaper peels, but we don't mind it,
In this cozy space, every mishap's the hit.
While the ceiling fan wobbles, the jokes start to flow,
As we tease the old vacuum—it's really quite slow!

The plants on the sill, are listening in,
With dirt on their leaves from the laughter within.
Each clink and each clatter brings cheer to the day,
In this quirky abode where we always will play.

Embracing the Everyday

In the corner, the cat takes a snooze,
While the dog plays the lead in the news.
A dance of dust bunnies swirls with flair,
As socks wander off, like they just don't care.

A sandwich sits proudly on the table's edge,
With crumbs as its friends, they form a hedge.
We laugh at the chaos, we grin at the view,
In this hodgepodge home, there's always a cue.

Touched by Time

The clock on the wall seems to giggle and sway,
Mocking my efforts to keep it at bay.
Old photos are laughing, with smiles so wide,
Revealing the secrets that time cannot hide.

A couch with a tale of adventures and spills,
The cushions conspire with mischievous thrills.
Every remote's gone rogue, hiding in flight,
In the quest for the movie, no one sleeps tight.

Alcove Whispers

In the nook, a plant has a story to share,
About nights full of snacks and a soft, cozy chair.
The curtains are peeking, they gossip and sigh,
As the sun does its dance, saying hello, goodbye.

A ball of yarn tangled in laughter and play,
With the puppy now wrestling, brightening the day.
We sip on our cocoa, with marshmallows afloat,
While the carpet, oh my, is holding a moat!

Footprints in Fabric

Each thread holds a story, a giggle, a glance,
Where slippers take journeys in a spirited dance.
The rug has seen spills of both juice and cheer,
And stories of friendships that thrive without fear.

A trail of mismatched socks leads to the door,
They've explored every corner, oh, what a tour!
With laughs that echo, the space comes alive,
In this cozy kingdom, it's fun to survive.

Nooks of Nostalgia

In corners filled with dust and dreams,
A cat's aloof, or so it seems.
We laugh at socks that never pair,
And find old toys in every chair.

The echoes of our silly fights,
Reappear like ghostly sights.
We dance around the spilled cold tea,
As laughter spills, wild and free.

Where memories hang like framed art,
Each joke a beat, each smile a part.
Echoes of childhood play,
In this quirky, fun display.

Canvas of Conversations

Painted walls hold whispered tales,
Of epic fails and shopping sales.
With every laugh, the colors grow,
A rainbow bright from toe to toe.

We chat of life, of dreams we'd chase,
A sneeze turns into a comic race.
From distant lands, absurd and grand,
Each story shared is richly planned.

A canvas stretched, so wide, so free,
In every corner, memory.
With each new tale, the laughter soars,
In this gallery, who needs doors?

A Tapestry of Togetherness

Woven threads of joy and jest,
In this space, we feel so blessed.
Each knot a tale of planned delight,
And every fray a comedy fight.

From board games lost to snacks devoured,
We find the fun, our inner powers.
As secrets shared in hushed surprise,
Unravel truths in goofy guise.

A tapestry of laughs and quirks,
Where every glance and giggle works.
In cozy nooks, our lives blend bright,
We twirl in chaos, pure delight.

Flickers of Familiarity

Light pops on like grand applause,
Laughter echoes; we pause, because,
The fridge door squeaks a silly tune,
As daylight wanes and night looms soon.

The creaky floorboards whisper why,
We sing along, we sing to the sky.
In familiar shadows, we play pretend,
Where every moment, laughter's friend.

Flickers dance like fireflies bright,
In this space, everything feels right.
Comfort abounds in every quirk,
With every laugh, together we smirk.

A Glimpse into Reverie

The cat's on the couch, snoozing in peace,
Dreaming of fish and a never-ending feast.
The dog peeks in with a curious glance,
Wondering why it's missing the dance.

A bird in the window begins to squawk,
Calling the cat for a chat and a talk.
But it's lost in its dream about giant mice,
A chase in the garden, oh would that be nice!

Steps into Sunlit Moments

The sun streams in with a golden beam,
Bouncing off toys, like a whimsical dream.
Kids tumble in, with giggles afloat,
While the dog plans a stealthy, slow boat.

Socks on the floor, it's a vibrant display,
Here lies the chaos of a glorious day.
Pizza crumbs sprinkled like stars on the rug,
Oh yes, this place is a cozy snug!

Frames of Unseen Stories

Picture frames hanging, dust on the glass,
Captured smiles, and growing up fast.
A missing shoe, claimed by the couch,
Who knew it was hiding? Oh, what a slouch!

The toast pops up with a sudden cheer,
Toasted to perfection, or nearly near.
A sticky note says, 'Lunch is on me!',
But little do they know, it's just last week's tea.

The Entry of Lost Laughter

In walks a friend wearing mismatched socks,
Trips on the rug, what a flurry of knocks!
With snacks in hand, it's a laughter parade,
As stories are shared, more memories made.

The plants look on with a jealous glare,
They wish to join in, if only aware.
But they stay put, in their pots with a sigh,
While laughter bounces, oh so high!

Comfort in the Corners

In the corner sits a chair,
With dust bunnies for a pair.
It tells tales of lazy days,
In mismatched socks and quirky ways.

A cat leaps up, all grace and skill,
Knocking over a cup with a thrill.
We laugh as it all goes tumbling down,
While the dog just rolls around, clowning about.

Hushed Conversations

In whispers behind the couch we scheme,
Sharing secrets like a daydream.
A snack raid planned, with stealth in mind,
While the snoozing cat's blissfully blind.

A sudden giggle, I try to shush,
But popcorn spills in an excited rush.
Laughter erupts, we cling to our chairs,
Wondering how we got into these snares.

The Gathering Place

Friends pile in, with shoes untied,
The sofa's now a wild slide.
We swap our snacks, a taste test fair,
Mismatched plates, a colorful affair.

A dance-off breaks out, all in good fun,
Spinning around, until we're done.
The laughter echoes, fills the room,
While the toaster smokes with impending doom!

Where Memories Dwell

Here's where we gather, in brilliant cheer,
Where every glance brings forth a tear.
With tales of mishaps from days gone by,
And pants that fit—just a lie!

Old photos laugh from the wall,
In sweaters that scream, 'We had a ball!'
We toast our past, with drinks in hand,
And dance like no one had ever planned.

Breaths of Domestic Grace

In slippers strange and mismatched socks,
I shuffle 'round and talk to clocks.
The dust bunnies hold secret rates,
As I negotiate with dinner plates.

My cat critiques with a judgmental stare,
While the couch claims spots for all who dare.
The fridge hums a sweet serenade,
As leftovers plan their grand parade.

A Doorway to Connection

Socks on the floor, a war zone declared,
In this kingdom of comfort, all's unprepared.
The TV storm brews a laugh-out-loud show,
While popcorn rains down in a buttery flow.

Friends gather round with snacks held tight,
Telling tales that last through the night.
Laughter bounces off every wall,
In this cherished ritual, we've built a hall.

Curiosities at the Threshold

Old shoes line up, they have their say,
Each tells a story of a different day.
A stray remote, a snack stash divine,
Together we chuckle at such a find.

The mailman knows more than he should,
He's seen my sofa, that's understood.
Jackets hanging, a whimsical art,
Each holds a memory, a giggle, a heart.

Familiar Faces and Forgotten Tales

Faces pop in like surprise party guests,
With tales of adventure and humorous quests.
A friend from the past with a potato sack,
He swears it's fashion, I might take it back.

Lemonade spills in a fit of glee,
As stories entwine like a tangled tree.
The warmth of laughter, the sound of cheer,
In this cozy space, life's magic is clear.

The Heart of the Home

The sofa's a throne, just like in a play,
Where socks hold court in a fanciful way.
The coffee pot's brewing a musical tune,
As crumbs hold a party, dancing under the moon.

The TV's a friend, though it's on the fritz,
It speaks in a language of laughs and of skits.
The remote's a magician, disappearing fast,
While the dog claims the cushion; oh, what a blast!

Spilled juice on the table, a sticky surprise,
While giggles erupt, and the cat rolls its eyes.
In this funny setup, we throw all our cares,
Creating sweet memories that float through the air.

Unfolding Dreams

In a corner, a blanket draped like a cape,
Turns the couch into castles, oh what an escape!
The pillows are clouds, soft and inviting,
As laughter erupts, our hearts are igniting.

The rug's a dance floor, where feet shoot and spin,
While snacks tell a story of crispy win-win.
We chase after dreams, with popcorn in hand,
Creating wild tales in our fun little land.

Footprints of pets leave their mark on the floor,
As everyone gathers, there's always room for more.
With giggles and chaos, oh what a delight,
In our lively kingdom, every day's a bright night.

Whispers of the Evening

As dusk paints the walls, the shadows arrive,
With whispers of mischief, they dance and they thrive.
The old clock is ticking, ticking just for fun,
While chairs join in laughter, 'til the day is done.

A bowl filled with treasures—snacks everyone seeks,
While the grandpa's old stories bring smiles, not leaks.
The curtains sway gently, in a playful breeze,
As secrets are shared between giggles and wheeze.

Laughter spills over like the drinks on the floor,
As late-night adventures just beckon for more.
In this cozy nook, where the evening unfolds,
We treasure these moments, worth more than pure gold.

Shadows on the Wall

With shadows a-dancing, they tease and they play,
On walls made of memories, brightening the way.
A mix-up of shoes leans against the chair,
As we share our tales in the soft evening air.

The plant in the corner wears a new hat,
While the family dog thinks he's part of the spat.
As the fridge hums a tune, we all take a seat,
Unraveling stories, no need to compete.

With laughter echoing, we sip from our cups,
Imagining a world where a duck quacks up.
In this cozy space, where giggles entwine,
The heart of the home—oh, what a divine!

The Threshold of Renewal

A knock, a laugh, they tumble in,
Chairs swallow them, where to begin?
Socks on the floor, a rogue cat strolls,
Chaos delights in our cozy shoals.

The coffee spills, a treacherous fate,
Pillows fly—all in good fate!
Head-scratchers shared at the snack break,
Who left the cake, for goodness' sake?

Giggles turn into games we churn,
The TV blares, and still we yearn.
A dance-off erupts on the rug,
One with grace, the other's a slug.

As laughter fades into the night,
We toast to chaos, hearts so light.
With opens doors and wit to lend,
Every visit feels like a bend.

Footprints on the Carpet

Tiny shoes and muddy paws,
A trail of fun without a pause.
What's that smell? Is it dessert?
Last week's leftovers, a gift or a hurt?

Jelly beans stuck to every chair,
A treasure hunt with plenty to share.
Grandma's knitting, a tangle of yarn,
Cats wielding strings, weaving their charm.

Under the table, giggles resound,
Footprints in cookie crumbs abound.
Chasing echoes, slipping with glee,
A parade of mischief, just let it be!

When night falls and smiles linger on,
We sigh at the mess, but it's a con.
For every footprint tells a tale,
Of laughter and joy—it will never pale.

Warmth from the Hearth

The fire crackles, stories ignite,
Marshmallows roast in the glow of light.
Funny faces, and jokes on tap,
We tumble within, like a cozy map.

In this warmth, all worries flee,
Even the dog claims a spot near me.
Grandpa dozes, but don't you wake—
He'll share secrets for old jokes' sake!

The cat thinks it's a fine old seat,
On my lap, purring soft and sweet.
Here's to chaos, to warmth and cheer,
With friends around, there's naught to fear!

As embers wink and the night unfolds,
Every chuckle, a story retold.
The hearth is a stage; join the fun,
Where laughter and warmth become one.

Visions Beyond the Welcome

Coming in with arms all wide,
A whirlwind of laughter, can't run or hide.
What's in the corner? A puzzle half-done,
Lost in the laughter, oh what fun!

A dance of mishaps, vibrant and true,
Jumping over toys as we all break through.
Can anyone dodge the rogue Lego block?
Priority one: avoid the shock!

The food table's a glorious sight,
With dishes stacked high—it's sheer delight!
Knock-knock jokes blend with tales of the wild,
In this crazy scene, we're all just a child.

So here we gather, in joy we dwell,
In this madcap haven, all is well.
Beyond the frames and walls we adore,
Are stories and laughter—who could want more?

Sentiments of the Entrance

Each time I enter, shoes in a mess,
I trip on the cat, oh what a stress.
The welcome mat smiles, it knows my plight,
It's a battle of wits, and I lose each night.

My coat hangs like a ghost on the rack,
Whispers of snacks call me with a smack.
The fridge hums a tune, it's simply a tease,
A dance with the leftovers, if you please.

Mirrors reflect all my quirks and blunders,
I laugh at the chaos while life quickly thunders.
A pile of junk mail becomes a grand throne,
In the kingdom of clutter, I'm never alone.

Each knock at the door has a story to tell,
From friendly surprise to that odd salesman's yell.
But oh, what delight when friends drop on by,
Laughter fills the air, soaring up to the sky.

The Embrace of Home's Heart

Home greets you warmly with a cheeky grin,
It knows all your secrets, all that you've been.
The couch conspires with pillows and throws,
To plot the best way to steal all your woes.

The doorbell sings like a cat seeking sun,
While I juggle my keys, laughing's begun!
The dog thinks he's king, a furry delight,
Stealing socks from the basket, a rogue in the night.

My slippers await, they're soft like a cloud,
As I slip into comfort, feeling so proud.
The fridge has a secret, a slice of cake calls,
Home is a wonderland where joy never stalls.

Each corner is cozy, crafted with cheer,
Memories echo, and trouble is mere.
Chaos is normal, a sidekick in glee,
In the embrace of warmth, I'm happy to be.

Finding Solace at the Door

With a turn of the knob, my adventures begin,
A world of surprises awaits from within.
The door creaks in laughter, a mischievous friend,
It knows all the big tales life loves to send.

From awkward first dates to loud family feasts,
Every moment shared becomes part of the beast.
The welcome sign lingers with a wink and a sigh,
As it watches the drama that passes it by.

Each arrival feels like a slapstick scene,
From shoes on the sofa to snacks barely seen.
The laughter bounces off walls painted bright,
While I dance with my troubles, oh what a sight!

Sometimes it's chaos, sometimes it's calm,
Yet each reunion feels like a spell and a charm.
So, here's to the door that swings wide with grace,
Where memories wander and joy finds its place.

The Corridor of Time

In the corridor where echoes delight,
Time flickers like candles in the soft night.
Each picture a story, a giggle, a tear,
Moments parade as the laughter draws near.

The clock ticks away in a comical race,
Reminding me daily of our wild, happy space.
As I dodge on the carpet, I pirouette low,
The dance of the hallway, a true comedy show.

Why is the cat always perched on the stairs?
Plotting to trip me while lounging in airs.
And the old chair squeaks like it knows my woes,
Yet it still supports me, as friendship bestows.

So, each trip to the door is a delightful chore,
Painting life's canvas with laughter galore.
In this corridor of time, we learn and we play,
Creating our stories in the silliest way.

Sounds of Comfort

A squeaky chair lets out a sigh,
While the cat leaps, oh my, oh my!
Remote controls lost in the fray,
Who took the last slice of dessert today?

The TV blares an old sitcom laugh,
Mom's making popcorn, oh what a path!
Kids giggle and race for the snack,
Beware the crumbs, they attack!

Socks on the floor create a maze,
Dance like a fool, let's set the world ablaze!
Laughter echoing in each nook,
Hold your sides, just take a look!

And as we settle with hearts so light,
In this wacky room, all feels right.
Laughter rings with every snort,
Who knew fun could be this short?

Reflections on the Coffee Table

A pile of magazines, stacked so high,
One falls down, oh, where'd it fly?
Coffee stains tell tales of yore,
   A spilled secret from before.

Coasters hide under cups and bowls,
Where's that puzzle? It rolls and rolls!
Sipping tea that's gone quite cold,
   Precious moments, easily sold.

Reflections shift from face to face,
   Someone's just lost their place!
A jigsaw piece under the chair,
What's that smell? Oh, is it fair?

We laugh and tease about the mess,
   But isn't this just sheer success?
With stories brewed over every sip,
The coffee table holds our fellowship.

Stories in Every Corner

Dust bunnies dance in the corner bright,
What a sight, oh what a fright!
Each chair tells tales of sitting too long,
With cushions that know we all belong.

Books piled high, some stacked askew,
Where's that novel? I thought I knew!
The lamp flickers, it's seen better days,
Chasing shadows in playful ways.

Old family photos, smiles so wide,
Captured moments on this wild ride.
A sock on the bookshelf, what a find,
In every corner, secrets unconfined!

We gather round, in fits of glee,
Telling tales, just you and me.
In this room, we spin like a wheel,
The stories shared become the real deal!

Nestled in Warmth

Cuddled close in soft embrace,
A blanket fort, a hidden space.
Chasing shadows with a flashlight beam,
In this nook, we start to dream.

Pizza crumbs on every plate,
Who could ask for a better fate?
Giggles burst like popcorn pops,
Our laughter dances, never stops.

Warmth of bodies, cozy tight,
Whispered secrets in the night.
A snore from Dad, a chuckle from Mum,
Ah, the joy of being so dumb!

Nestled in fun, we doze and sigh,
Time flies past, oh my, oh my!
In this warmth, our spirits soar,
Who needs a stage when life's the score?

Beyond the Entryway

A cat in a box, what a sight,
It thinks it's a queen, oh what a delight.
Socks on the floor, a puzzling maze,
Tripping, I'm laughing, lost in a daze.

The couch is a pirate ship, I'm the crew,
With a dog as my matey, we drift the blue.
Waves of popcorn, splashed on the wall,
We cheer for the fish, who swim and stall.

Chairs left spinning, a game on the run,
Round and round, oh, so much fun!
My feet are the engines, my hands the sails,
We're off to hunt for forgotten tales.

The doorbell rings, who could it be?
A pizza delivery? Just for me!
The laughter spills out, like a bubbly drink,
Life's little moments, make me rethink.

Secrets in the Lounge

In the corner, a plant, with secrets to share,
It listens to gossip while sitting there.
Coasters with stains from drinks long gone,
Got stories of parties that linger on.

The remote plays hide-and-seek with me,
Under cushions, it's where it likes to be!
Suddenly spotted, it jumps back in place,
A game of chance in the daily race.

A mirror reflects all the chaos we bring,
It giggles softly at the silly bling.
A vase tipped over after a wild cheer,
Leaves us laughing, forgetting the fear.

Then comes the dog, with a joyful bark,
Chasing his tail, creating a spark.
In this cozy space, with laughter and cheer,
We find our secrets, year after year.

Framed Moments of Light

On the wall hang photos, a mismatched set,
Grandma's wide smile, can't forget!
The frames are crooked, but it feels just right,
In each captured moment, there's vivid delight.

A tiny handprint, a story untold,
Reminds us of laughter, and memories bold.
Next to it, a gift from the neighbor's cat,
A smudge on the glass, where it once sat.

Days turn to nights, and time seems to play,
With stories in shadows that dance and sway.
A toddler's giggle, the dog's sudden leap,
Is all it takes to stir laughter from sleep.

With friends around, the stories unwind,
Shared in the light, in unison, entwined.
In these framed moments, we find our bliss,
Each giggle and glance, a treasure we won't miss.

Echoes of Laughter

On a rainy day, we gather inside,
With a deck of cards, let the games abide.
Each hand brings a chuckle, and silly bluffs,
In the battle for chips, no one plays tough.

The fridge opens wide, a snack attack,
Popcorn and cookies, there's never a lack.
We munch and we crunch, as jokes fill the air,
In a contest of who can do the funniest flair.

An accidental spill, a chorus of squeals,
With laughter like bubbles, it's joy that appeals.
The cat steals a treat, then darts for the door,
Leaving us gasping, then begging for more.

As evening settles, we replay our day,
With echoes of laughter, they softly sway.
In this cozy haven, our hearts feel alive,
Where each silly moment helps us thrive.

Between the Pillows

In the fluff of cushions, a snack lies still,
A brave cracker trying to escape the grill.
The remote is hiding, too shy to be found,
While the cat acts like she owns the whole ground.

A sock flies out, a launch from the seat,
Trying to dodge, a tangled retreat.
Game night has started, chaos galore,
With laughter erupting from just next door.

The dog takes a nap, on top of my feet,
While we plot the next round of snacks to eat.
An intermission call, to chase wayward fries,
Smuggling chips like a thief in disguise.

In the midst of the laughter, the bubble does pop,
As I trip on a toy while dodging the mop.
A tumble, a laugh—oh, what a delight!
Where fun hides so simply, in plain sight.

The Art of Welcome

A knock at the door, it's the neighbor again,
With baked goods that smell like they're heaven's own kin.
A warm plate exchanged, with laughter that flows,
As we sip on tea that nobody knows.

"Have you seen my dog?"—oh, the games we play,
He's hiding inside like he's on holiday.
With a wag of the tail and a leap off the couch,
He claims all the attention, our little wild grouch.

The walls hold memories of friends long gone,
And every soft chuckle is part of our song.
A cactus in hand, they comment with glee,
"Here's a housewarming gift! Will it prick you or me?"

As we munch through the chaos, the mishaps begin,
The casserole's singing, "Will we ever fit in?"
But with joy and a gridlock of jokes in the air,
It's the art of welcome we find everywhere.

Embracing the Ordinary

The daily grind wears a silly hat,
As I dance with the dishes and play with the cat.
A sock puppet show from the folds of the chair,
'Cause normal can always use a bit of flair.

Chores march like soldiers, in perfect line,
But with a little mischief, they're suddenly fine.
I sing to the broom, twirl around the floor,
A choreographed number I call 'Chores-A-Plenty' encore.

The vacuum's a partner in this wacky show,
Chasing after crumbs like it's some wild rodeo.
While laundry has secrets, little socks go stray,
Guess the dryer is hosting a sock cabaret.

In the simplest moments, I find my delight,
A pinch of the mundane makes everything bright.
So here's to the chaos, the giggles, the mess,
In the dance of the ordinary, we always feel blessed.

Vignettes from the Hearth

Dinner's a circus, the peas roll away,
A race on the table, who'll eat the most play?
Mom's got her apron, and dad's got the grin,
But somehow the dog is the one who will win.

The story unfolds of a family so dear,
With anecdotes shared over each hearty cheer.
Grandma's old tale of the pie gone astray,
Still makes us laugh till the end of the day.

With candles aglow, and the music just right,
We share all our secrets, our fears, and our light.
There's giggles, there's sighs, with a sprinkle of love,
As the hearth warms our hearts, like a fire from above.

In each little vignette, the laughter persists,
From spills on the table to unplanned twists.
These snapshots of life, oh so whimsically cast,
In the homey embrace, let the good times last.

Mapping the Moments

We gather here to share our tales,
With laughter bouncing off the walls.
The dog decides to steal the snacks,
While the cat just rolls and sprawls.

Friends spill secrets, silly and bright,
While we argue over the last slice.
A dance-off breaks out, what a sight,
And the couch just starts to suffice.

A game of charades goes awry,
As Aunt Betty pretends to fly.
The popcorn turns into a fight,
And we end up laughing 'til we cry.

The Spirit of Togetherness

We gather round in mismatched seats,
With pizza toppings all amiss.
The remote's lost under the treats,
As we chase each other for a bliss.

Grandpa tells a joke that's so old,
We can't help but laugh through our groans.
A dance party breaks, and we unfold,
Hoping to skip the sappy tones.

The kids run wild, wearing socks for hats,
While the dog plays referee in between.
Stories fly like sprightly bats,
As we toast to moments unforeseen.

Where Hearts Converge

In this circle, we play and tease,
The floor's a dance stage, no one's shy.
We make a mess, we spark and freeze,
With mismatched socks being the style to fly.

The coffee's spilled, paint on the wall,
As we share memories like a prank.
A slight chance of laughter in the hall,
The hand-me-down jokes, a colorful tank.

Voices blend, like tunes on air,
With fake awards for best routine.
The clock ticks by, but we don't care,
In this realm, we reign supreme.

Bowls of Stories

A bowl of chips, a bowl of cheer,
As we sit and plot our next big prank.
Dramatic flair with every cheer,
In this capsule where we maintain a rank.

Our stories twist like vines in spring,
With hand gestures that grow quite large.
Laughter erupts like a wild fling,
With snacks acting as our launch pad charge.

Tales of faux pas, silly and grand,
We swirl them round like a dance of fire.
Connection flows, a gentle hand,
With every laugh, we rise higher.

The Fabric of Family

In the corner, socks take flight,
A cat is wrestling with delight.
Grandpa's snoring makes a sound,
As chaos swirls all around.

Mom's lost her keys—could they be?
In the fridge? Or stuck in a tree?
Laughter echoes, spills like tea,
In this quilt of love, wild and free.

Sister's dance breaks every rule,
While Dad claims he's the best at school.
A bed becomes a trampoline,
In this crazy family scene.

Nothing's perfect, but that's okay,
We find the joy in our own way.
Jelly stains and crayon art,
Bright threads weave into the heart.

A Halo of Affection

A hound in sunglasses likes to pose,
While Grandma's plant prefers to doze.
Silly hats adorn our heads,
As laughter tumbles from our beds.

With tickle fights that leave us sore,
And jokes that land with perfect score.
All is right when we convene,
A family unit always keen.

Dad's attempts at magic tricks,
End in giggles, fails, and kicks.
A pineapple wears a cozy scarf,
With love that makes us always laugh.

In our bubble, joy is near,
Every smile, a souvenir.
In this space, affection's bright,
Like stars that twinkle in the night.

Hearthstones of History

Witness to the crazed ballet,
The popcorn's flying, come what may.
Someone's foot gets caught in the chair,
As giggles float right through the air.

Old photos tell tales of our past,
Like dinosaurs on a fridge so vast.
Grandpa sports a laughable mustache,
While Grandma bakes her famous hash.

Between the crumbs of snacks long past,
We swear next time we'll eat more fast.
Cards and games turn serious quick,
On the floor a tic-tac-toe brick.

Echoes of laughter, a sweet refrain,
Of shenanigans that drive us insane.
This hearth of warmth holds us tight,
As history dances in the light.

Fragments of Daylight

The couch is a mountain, pillows are peaks,
On royal thrones, each one speaks.
Frisbees fly and kids collide,
In our playroom, fun will abide.

When Dad trips on a rogue toy car,
We gather 'round and cheer à la char.
A flying snack attacks from afar,
It's like the scene of a wild bazaar.

Mom's creating a culinary dream,
While we devise a sticky scheme.
Jelly fingers paint the wall,
As laughter catches—who holds the ball?

With every fragment lit by sun,
We capture moments, just for fun.
This wacky dance of love and play,
Makes every evening like a holiday.

The Heartbeat of Habitats

In the corner, a cat sprawls wide,
Dreaming of mice on a fluffy ride.
Socks strewn about like confetti,
A floor party, oh so petty!

The TV blares our favorite show,
While the dog sniffs what lies below.
Spills and thrills, unplanned events,
Every slip brings laughter tense!

A pizza box, a shocking find,
Half a crust, a party unconfined.
Remote control on the ceiling fan,
How did that get there? No one can plan!

Memories tucked under the couch,
Echoes of laughter, every blouch.
This is home, where silly reigns,
In absurdity, joy remains!

A Canvas of Togetherness

Paint splotches splashed on the floor,
Art attack? A need for more!
A canvas made of love and mess,
Life's masterpiece in sweet distress.

The toddler now daubs with glee,
While grandpa snores beneath the tree.
"A masterpiece!" we boldly say,
As we step back and shout hooray!

Sticky fingers, pots of glue,
Our gallery? Just for a few.
Each stroke tells a story so bright,
Of laughter echoing through the night.

"Mom, I'm an artist," declares the child,
While dad's in a corner, running wild.
Together we create, side by side,
This joyful chaos, our hearts collide!

Windows to the Soul

Peeking out, the flowers sway,
A curious squirrel starts to play.
Bathed in sun, the colors glow,
   Silly antics steal the show.

The neighbors argue, who knew why?
Came home late, a smirk in their eye.
We giggle behind the frosted glass,
Eavesdropping on their evening class.

A child yells, "I want my snack!"
Mom replies, "You're on the right track!"
Echoing laughter, the shared delight,
   Life outside is pure, just right.

So we open wide the blinds each day,
For nature's show and quirky play.
In this space, our love gets whole,
Through life's window, peeks the soul!

Embracing the Familiar

Old slippers worn, they hug my feet,
A little too snug, but they're so sweet.
Couch cushions toss, a temporary throne,
In my realm of cozy, I'm never alone.

A mug of cocoa, whipped cream delight,
Sipping warm, oh what a sight!
The TV crackles, all shows rewind,
Napping in layers, unconfined.

Grandma's blanket draped on the chair,
Wrapped in love, with a little flair.
The scent of cookies wafts through the air,
A sweet embrace that always cares.

So we gather, this quirky clan,
Finding laughter where life's unplanned.
With each heartbeat in this space we share,
Familiar love is beyond compare!

Invitations to the Heart's Sanctuary

Come one, come all, to this cozy spree,
Where socks go missing, and cats sip tea.
The couch is a tangle of snacks and cheer,
Even the plants giggle; they're happy here.

We've got jokes tucked in the cushions galore,
And pillows that bounce with a light-hearted roar.
Unplug your worries, let laughter unfold,
In this heart's sanctuary, we're rich, not sold.

Grab a snack; just watch out for the crumbs,
As laughter erupts, a parade of funny puns.
The door to this joy is always ajar,
Let the comedians enter; we'll be the stars.

So join in the fun, don't hesitate,
For joy has a way of crafting fate.
In this room of giggles, your heart takes flight,
Welcome to hilarity on this fine night.

The Threshold of Dreams

Step right up to the land of surprise,
Where slippers do dance and old chairs do rise.
The cat spins tales of her nightly quest,
While the dog snores dreams of being the best.

Here's a place where the odd socks roam,
In cozy corners, they've made their home.
The refrigerator hums a soft-late tune,
As the cookies plot schemes by the bright yellow moon.

Grab some giggles; they're free to take,
Don't mind the floor; it likes to shake.
Each threshold crossed is a new escapade,
Where every laugh is a choice you've made.

The couch is a cloud, the carpet a sea,
In this sea of silliness, come sail with me.
Our dreams float high, just like our song,
Welcome to a place where you truly belong!

Awakened Spaces

Hello to the morning, the sun's on its way,
Where laughter and coffee blend bright with the day.
The otter pajamas whisper soft, 'Let's play!'
As breakfast debates if it's time to stay.

Cushions conspire, mere mortals beware,
This room's got secrets that float in the air.
The spider webs sparkle, they're party confetti,
While the vacuum cleaner's more dodgy than steady.

Awaken the giggles that hide in the nooks,
The toaster's got toast; it's reading the books.
Join the confection that bounces with flair,
As joy fills the spaces like fresh spring air.

Oh come one, come all, to this joyful place,
Where everyone's welcome, and smiles embrace.
These spaces are waiting, with open arms too,
A carnival of laughter, just here for you!

Keyhole Glimpses

Peeking through corners where mischief does bloom,
There's giggles a-tripping from this funny room.
The kettle's whistling, a curious song,
As the clock does a tango, a true dance along.

What's that hiding behind the old chair?
A sock puppet stretching, with dreams to share.
The cat curtsies low, and the dog takes a bow,
In this delightful chaos, oh where to now?

Cracked mugs tell tales of beverages spilled,
While the crumbs on the counter feel oddly thrilled.
A peek through the keyhole reveals all the fun,
Where every old item is crafty and spun.

So glimpse a bit closer, and you'll start to see,
The funny that dances, oh so carefree.
In this chamber of comedy, nothing feels wrong,
Invite yourself in; let's sing a new song!

Tides of Togetherness

A cat with a mission, quite quite absurd,
Wanders the rug like a king undeterred.
The couch creaks under laughter and cheer,
While spilled popcorn pops up like tiny pioneers.

Grandma's old sweater, a treasure of guise,
Worn with flair like a crown in disguise.
We dance with the dust bunnies under the light,
As the clock chimes for dinner, we'miss quite the sight.

The TV remote, that slippery sprite,
Hides in the cushions—oh what a delight!
We're all on a quest, armed with our snacks,
Like pirates in search of forgotten blackbacks.

And as night wraps its arms around our wild play,
We collapse on the couch, what a curious day!
In ties of togetherness, laughing we sigh,
A bond woven tightly, it'll never run dry.

A Seat by the Fire

A seat by the fire, the cat claims it first,
His purring so constant, it's quite like a verse.
The marshmallows roast with a comical flare,
While we watch as they tumble, a sweetened despair.

Dad tells a tale, which somehow goes wrong,
With pirates and treasure, but much more a song.
Mom rolls her eyes, as she stirs the pot slow,
Saying, 'Last time I checked, he's just a fellow!'

The logs crackle loudly, the shadows dance bright,
While we poke at the embers that twinkle in sight.
Someone sneezes loudly, it echoes, a sneeze!
And the cat jumps as if swarmed by bubbles, oh please!

In warmth and in laughter, that seat feels just right,
It's here where we gather, sharing our night.
With stories and giggles, the moments take flight,
By the fire's sweet glow, everything feels light.

Candles and Memories

Candles flicker gently, casting odd shapes,
While we gather around telling silly escapes.
The cake's a surprise, with icing askew,
And laughter erupts, like a burst of bright dew.

Uncle Joe tries a dance, that has no rhythm,
With moves that defy the laws of all wisdom.
We cheer him on, with a chorus quite grand,
'For the moves of your youth, oh do take a stand!'

The stories we share, both silly and sweet,
Like the time that a goat turned our picnic to neat.
With each candle's glow, a memory wakes,
As we hoot and we holler, for goodness sakes!

So here's to the candles, the laughter anew,
The memories we cherish, and all that we do.
Through each flickering flame, comes a smile wide,
For the moments we treasure, we'll always confide.

Glimpses of the Everyday

Glimpses of the day, through the windows it beams,
A dog in the sunshine, dreaming up dreams.
Mom wrestles with laundry, oh where does it go?
While Dad reads the paper, turned upside down, oh no!

A spill on the table, glue sticks in hand,
Art projects strewn like a post-it note band.
The kids make a fortress with blankets stretched wide,
As they plot to invade with giggles and pride.

The fridge hums a tune, matching our song,
As we load up on snacks, 'Bigger bites, not wrong!'
And the clock ticks on by, a gentle old friend,
Reminding us softly, the worries will mend.

In glimpses of laughter, we catch fleeting sights,
Of everyday magic, oh such joyous flights!
For life's in the moments, both mundane and bold,
Where all of our stories are brilliantly told.

Windows to Yesterday

Peeking through the glass frame,
A squirrel steals my snack game.
Mom's laughter fills the air,
As dad's dance moves give a scare.

Old photos hang on the wall,
Uncle Fred's jumps, watch him fall!
Time travelers in our cheer,
Making memories far and near.

Sister's sock, a lost decoy,
Hidden prize for little joy.
Cat's on guard, a mischief spree,
Paws on the couch, oh what glee!

But wait, the fridge is calling me,
A jigsaw puzzle's half-done spree.
Come back, my friends, let's play some more,
Adventures are waiting behind that door.

Memories in the Hallway

Echoes dance upon the floor,
Onward to the kitchen door.
A runaway sock, what a sight!
Mom thinks she's the fashion light.

Chasing shadows on the wall,
Whispers loud, we heed their call.
An ancient vase could tell a tale,
Of epic battles, thanks to mail!

Grandpa's chair, a throne so grand,
Pillow fights as we make a stand.
Tickling fights and silly grins,
This hallway where the laughter spins.

A door that creaks with every step,
Time-traveling with each careful prep.
We won't forget this playful space,
Where giggles thrive and woes erase.

The Path of Daily Rituals

Coffee brewing, toast on fire,
Dad's unique method inspires.
Mom escapes with her big mug,
While we cheer her on, snug as a bug.

Sister's antics with the cat,
Swiping toys, imagine that!
The daily race to grab the last,
A breakfast battle—who will outlast?

Jokes shared over plates that clink,
Spilled juice makes the kitchen stink.
But laughter drowns the mess we make,
These morning moments, a precious cake.

With chatter buzzing like a bee,
Rituals wrapped in harmony.
We'll hold this chaos, warmth in store,
Knowing love's the richest score.

Dreams Beneath the Archway

Under arches, where shadows play,
We sketch our dreams in the clay.
The broom left leaning, oh so sly,
A playful ghost, where whispers fly.

In the corner, treasures hide,
Foundling books and dog jokes tried.
Magical lands and wizards here,
Each tale told brings us near.

The rug has seen a thousand spins,
With each tumble, laughter wins.
Underfoot, forgotten cheer,
Echoes of joy from yesteryear.

A door left ajar, a wink, a smile,
Every inch we map, worth our while.
In this space, we invent, explore,
Building dreams, oh evermore.

Portraits of Serenity

A cat in a sunbeam, sprawled and divine,
Dreaming of tuna, oh what a line!
The dog in the corner, with socks held so dear,
Guarding his treasures, it's perfectly clear.

Mom's on the couch, with a bowl full of snacks,
Remote in her hand, she's ready with hacks.
Dad in the kitchen, concocting a dish,
It's more smoke than food—oh, how I wish!

Kids chase each other, a giggle parade,
While the plants on the shelf seem slightly afraid.
The clock hands go round, like dancers in trance,
Every moment's a party, who needs pants?

Yet through all the chaos, the laughter ignites,
In this living room scene, everything's right.
A wild tapestry, woven with fun,
In these portraits of peace, life's never done.

Under the Glow

Beneath the soft lights, the shadows do brawl,
While the dog snorts and snores, we stand proud and tall.
Spilled popcorn on floors, a treasure we find,
Dancing like children, unburdened, unlined.

A game of charades, oh what a sight,
Dad's moves are so wild, he gives us a fright!
Mom's laughter erupts, it echoes for miles,
While uncle Fred's jokes are more cringe than smiles.

Curtains are swaying, a breeze sweeps away,
All our grown-up woes, come join in the play.
Tangled up in laughter, wrinkles and glee,
Under the glow, it's just you and me.

So let's toast with our mugs, to evenings like these,
Where silliness reigns, and we're all just at ease.
This under-the-glow magic, a timeless delight,
Where every dumb moment feels perfectly right.

Sighs of Contentment

On the couch sat a dog, his belly quite round,
Sighing so deeply, the loudest of sounds.
While the kids pull his ears, he just rolls his eyes,
Living the life, he's a master of sighs.

A popcorn incident, kernels in hair,
As mom laughs it off, without any care.
Dad's in the kitchen, inventing new things,
Each dish that he makes, has its own set of wings.

Twinkling fairy lights make the room glow bright,
Chasing shadows that dance in the dim light.
Each sigh a reminder of simple joys now,
In this laughter-filled sanctuary, take a bow.

To all our small moments, let's raise up a cheer,
For giggles and joys, andffestive family cheer.
In the sighs of contentment, our hearts truly soar,
In this cozy abode, we always want more.

Shelters of Solace

A slip on the rug, oh what a great fall,
Laughter erupting, that's the best call!
With pillows and blankets, a fortress quite neat,
We battle with laughter—what a fun feat!

Kids building towers, of couch cushions high,
While the cat takes a nap, with a disgruntled sigh.
Each block that they stack gets critiqued with a grin,
"Watch out for the fortress, our fun's about to begin!"

The TV blares loud, as we shout and we cheer,
For every small victory, we all hold so dear.
In this refuge so warm, we find our own way,
With goofy little moments, brightening the day.

In shelters of solace, our hearts all align,
Finding joy in the chaos, sip on that sunshine.
With laughter and love, we create our own lore,
In this grand family home, who could ask for more?

The Portal to Nostalgia

A carpet worn from many feet,
A place where old memories meet.
Lurking cats with royal airs,
Plotting schemes 'neath vacant chairs.

Toys that squeak and giggle loud,
Once the pride of every crowd.
Now they linger, dusted gray,
In corners where the shadows play.

A door that creaks with every sway,
As if to whisper, "Come and stay!"
Life's distractions drift and curl,
In this funny, twirling whirl.

A sofa that swallows every guest,
Who leaves behind their Sunday best.
And echoes of laughter, bright and clear,
Float around, like memories dear.

Echoes in the Foyer

A coat rack holds a wizard's cloak,
Or maybe just an old dad's joke.
Shoes that tell of journeys grand,
Each pair loves to make a stand.

The mirror reflects a silly face,
Posed in some ridiculous space.
Footsteps sound like giggles near,
Echoing fun, oh so clear!

A potted plant with wilting grace,
Wonders who took the prime space.
Yet here we dance, our hearts in sync,
In memory's brew, we share a wink.

The entry whispers tales of cheer,
Of friends who've come and brought good beer.
Each laugh a note in this sweet score,
Replaying times we can't ignore.

Secrets Behind the Curtain

A tangled web of threads and dreams,
Where nothing's quite as easy as it seems.
Behind the drapes, a cat takes flight,
Chasing dust motes in the light.

The old television hums a tune,
Of sitcoms long past, beneath the moon.
Faded memories wrapped tight and warm,
Like sweaters knit to keep us calm.

The cushions giggle when you sit,
Hiding secrets, just a bit.
Once a throne of grandeur bright,
Now a stage for silly fights.

Each shadow spins a yarn to tell,
Of laughter's rise and the occasional yell.
Behind those curtains, all is fun,
In this place where time is spun.

The Passage to Familiarity

A hallway echoes with lost tales,
Of family trips and wildails.
Framed pictures watch with knowing eyes,
As if to say, "No need for lies."

The squeaky floorboards speak of glee,
As children dash like bumblebees.
Each thump and crash, a vibrant score,
In the passageway we all adore.

A collection of oddments all around,
Curiosities that make us sound.
A rubber chicken, a broken clock,
What's that? Oh! Another sock!

In this space, we find our way,
With laughter lighting up the gray.
Familiarity's warm embrace,
In these little joys, we find our place.

A Journey in the Foyer

I tripped on a shoe, then a cat,
Spinning 'round like a circus acrobat.
A dance with the coat rack, oh what a sight,
Who knew a foyer could spark such delight?

Footprints of snacks left a trail of crumbs,
Are those little feet or a pack of hungry bums?
My keys on a table, lost 'neath the fluff,
Why is it that finding them's always so tough?

The doorbell's a joker, it plays hide and seek,
Every time it rings, I jump like a freak.
With laughter and chaos, it fills the air,
In the foyer of fun, there's never a care.

So here's to the entry, where mischief abounds,
With tales of mishaps and playful sounds.
Each step in this space, a whimsical chore,
A journey of joy in the house's core.

Sunlight's Embrace

Sunbeams burst in to tickle my toes,
Chasing the shadows and warming my nose.
With a giggle, the curtains begin to sway,
As if they're dancing in a bright ballet.

A sunny spot's claimed by the old dog's leap,
In a heap of fur, he's lost in his sleep.
Whiskers twitch softly, dreaming of bones,
In the sunlit haven, all fear is overthrown.

The potted plant sneezes, dust in the air,
Each leaf has its secrets, though nobody cares.
A sunbeam's embrace, oh what a delight,
It turns the mundane into sheer light.

So here in this warmth, laughter takes flight,
Every corner's a canvas, painted with light.
In this moment of bliss, joy finds its place,
In a sunny embrace, there's love and grace.

Reflections of Us

Mirrors all laughing with a wink and a grin,
Showing our quirks, the chaos within.
We strike silly poses, oh what a view,
A gallery of goofballs, me and you.

The couch is a stage, and we're the stars,
With popcorn explosions and chocolaty bars.
We act like children with giggles so grand,
Creating our sitcom, oh, isn't it planned?

The floor's a trampoline, we bounce just like kids,
Dodging the laundry, oh, where have they hid?
In the funhouse of life, we dance and we play,
Our reflections show joy in the silliest way.

So let's pop the popcorn and turn up the show,
In this home full of laughter, love will always grow.
With each mirrored moment, a treasure disguised,
Reflections of us, the best kind of prize.

The Portal to Serendipity

A quirky entry that twists like a rhyme,
Each step is a journey, an adventure in time.
My sock's on the ceiling, a lost, funny friend,
In this silly doorway, the surprises won't end.

Brooms lean like spies, they plot and they scheme,
While the vacuum hums softly, lost in a dream.
The door swings wide, trapping giggles inside,
With laughter erupting, there's nowhere to hide.

Behind every shoe lies a story untold,
Of mischief and memories, brave and bold.
With each friendly knock, a wild guest appears,
The portal to serendipity brings all the cheers.

So here's to the laughter that's found on the way,
In a world built of whimsy, we laugh and we play.
Each moment a treasure, in chaos we thrive,
In this joyful space, it's where we come alive!

The Rhythm of Home

In the cozy nook, the cat takes a leap,
Chasing dust bunnies, in a playful sweep.
The coffee pot gurgles, tunes of the day,
While socks on the floor join in the ballet.

With laughter and chaos, the kids start to sing,
Mismatched socks dance, oh what a thing!
The couch is a ship, sailing to lands,
With pirates and dragons, all at our hands.

The door creaks open, what will we find?
A dog with a shoe? Oh dear, never mind!
In this wacky world, there's never a bore,
The jester is here, what's behind that door?

So raise up your cups, let's toast to the fun,
In this rhythm of life, we'll never be done.
With quirks and with laughs, our hearts are a score,
Together we thrive, forever, encore!

In the Lap of Familiarity

The radio crackles, a tune from the past,
Dancing with pops, oh how it contrasts!
The sofa's a sea, where we drift and float,
With snacks piled high, we find joy in the moat.

A statue of a gnome winks with delight,
His garden of joy sparkles in the night.
The fridge hums a melody, cold and sweet,
While leftovers are treasures we're eager to greet.

The walls hold our laughter, a cozy embrace,
Each picture a tale, time cannot erase.
From spilled grape juice to crumbs on the floor,
Life's little messes, we can't help but adore.

So here's to the giggles, the quirks we embrace,
In the lap of this home, we've found our place.
With love that grows fonder, like a well-worn shoe,
Every day brings a dance, and it's all just for you.

Comfort's Embrace

Under warm blankets, we nest and we snuggle,
Rummaging for chocolate, oh sweet little trouble!
The TV's on mute, but the laughter is loud,
As we share silly stories, our little crowd.

The cushions are castles, cushions are thrones,
With battles and hugs, we conquer the zones.
The plants give a nod, they're part of the crew,
In this crazy kingdom, where dreams all come true.

The spoons in the drawer spin tales of their own,
Whispers of curry, and noodle-filled home.
Wobbling dinner plates, all stacked in a row,
Like dancers at a party, they put on a show.

So bring on the chaos, the mess we adore,
In comfort's embrace, we always want more.
With love like a blanket, warm as the sun,
Every mishap a riot, every hug full of fun.

A Sense of Belonging

The slippers yell 'hello' as I walk on through,
Each step feels like home, cozy and true.
The clutter sings songs of a life lived with flair,
What's that on the carpet? A slice of old pear?

In the corners, there's laughter, echoes of cheer,
The potted plant stretches, saying, "You're here!"
Each trinket a treasure, a story to share,
As we weave our own tapestry, stitched with care.

The clock ticks and tocks, keeping time with a grin,
Mixing seconds with memories, where chaos begins.
With each little moment, we find our true song,
In this quirky abode where we all belong.

So let's gather our treasures, our giggles, our noise,
Together we shine, both the girls and the boys.
With hearts intertwined in this beautiful dance,
Here's to the laughter that gives life a chance!

Tales from the Couch

On cushions we gather, a sight so absurd,
With snacks in hand, the couch may curd.
A cat takes a leap, misses the mark,
And lands in the chips, oh what a spark!

Remote in one hand, a soda in the other,
We argue 'bout movies like each is a brother.
With laughter erupting, the dog snorts and rolls,
As one sneezes loudly, we all lose control!

That old couch is a ship on a sea of fluff,
With stories aplenty and giggles enough.
Elevated feet and slippers galore,
Every night's magic behind this thick door!

And when finally tired, we collapse in a heap,
Belly laughs linger as we drift into sleep.
Tomorrow once more, the tales will resume,
In this kingdom of comfort, it's hard to feel gloom!

An Invitation to Tranquility

In the afternoon glow, we recline with ease,
Where the clock ticks slowly and worries freeze.
A tumbleweed rolls, oh wait, it's just pet hair,
Silly reminders of life's lively affair.

A cup of tea spills, rains on the floor,
Oh, laugh it off, what's a few puddles more?
We debate the best blanket for a cozy film,
While arguments fly, it's all part of the whim!

As shadows creep in, we avoid the chat,
About dinners we've burnt or the time with the cat.
Pizza boxes stacked, a real-life art piece,
An exhibition on chaos, but the mood's full of peace.

So let's toast to this couch, the throne of our fun,
Where stories and laughter are never outrun.
In this simple space, joy finds its way,
An invitation to chill, come and laugh, let's play!

Portraits in Stillness

We sit like statues, each with our blend,
Of leftovers from lunch that we love to defend.
A curious dog peeks from under the chair,
Debating if snatching is worth the risk there.

Dad's in a slumber, off chasing his dreams,
While the kids build castles; so silly it seems.
Mom's tracking the latest buzz on her phone,
In a world of her own, yet not quite alone.

The walls echo laughter, a paint job of cheer,
With memories growing each time we gather near.
Feet up on the table, the coffee looks grand,
In this gallery of life, it's the best we've planned!

As night falls around us, the couch holds our tales,
Of mishaps and giggles, like whimsical sails.
Each portrait a moment, each laugh is a brush,
In the stillness, we find joy, as we savor the hush.

The Melody of Gathering

With friends by the couch, a raucous delight,
We feast on the chips, a crunchy good bite.
The dog on the rug steals glances of hope,
As laughter erupts, we're all on this rope.

Each voice a unique note, a fantastic tune,
As stories collide under the light of the moon.
One joke leads to another, like a dance that we weave,
In this melody of life, it's fun to believe.

Napkins turned blankets; we lounge with a grin,
Games of charades bring the giggles within.
An old flick plays on, much to our glee,
Where dialogue's cheesy and hearts roam free!

As the night carries on, with snacks on our laps,
We cherish these moments, this joy that unwraps.
A symphony of laughter, a chorus that roars,
In the warmth of this space, we are always yours!